The Cathedral

The Baptistery
and the Campanile

Gabriella Di Cagno

The Cathedral

The Baptistery and the Campanile

Mandragora

50122 Firenze - Piazza Duomo 9
www.mandragora.it

Grafica: Lorenzo Gualtieri
Fotografie: Andrea Bazzechi
Massimo Sestini, p. 96
Raffaello Bencini, p. 95
Stampa: ABC Tipografia, Sesto Fiorentino
ISBN 88-85957-41-2

The importance and responsability of the Cathedral Authorities of Santa Maria del Fiore are clear when one considers the importance of the historical and cultural heritage represented by this artistic complex. For seven centuries it has worked to protect, preserve and maintain this group of buildings which is so precious and so attractive to an ever increasing number of visitors and residents, concerned and desirous of enriching their own cultural knowledge. Others simply wish to participate in retrospect - if only for a brief moment - in the wonderful artistic flowering which Florence witnessed and which we should all be proud to protect.

Dr. U. TAFANI
President of the Opera
di Santa Maria del Fiore

It is really rather difficult to synthesize the history and facts relevant to these important monuments for the visitor. Piazza San Giovanni (or Piazza del Duomo) is, in fact, a treasure trove not just of art and history, but also of political and civil life. It is without doubt one of the oldest and most important areas of the city. The three buildings, (Cathedral, Campanile and Baptistery) linked by various historical and artistic events, formed one large building site where artists and intellectuals were able to work together to their mutual benefit. Many artists worked here in their youth, serving their apprenticeship before becoming famous themselves.
It is possible to identify within the main building site, (in other words the Cathedral, Campanile and Baptistery), actual 'sub-sites', for example that of the 'Porta della Mandorla', or the Cathedral dome, or the lantern. These are particular areas where work took longer and involved various artists, often employed as the result of a competition.

(School of) Bernardo Daddi, Madonna della Misericordia, Bigallo Museum.

After the three monuments, one should visit the Museo dell'Opera del Duomo (Cathedral Museum), for it is here that many of the original works are kept, as well as many which, for reasons of conservation, have been removed from their original location, but are now well displayed in an arrangement which, as far as possible, reflects their original position.
The present day aspect of both Cathedral and Baptistery differs considerably from their original appearance. Some of the changes are slight, - statues and relief sculptures, or doors, have been moved from one side to another, altars and other structures have been built and then removed. Other changes however, have been enormous, - such as the demolition of entire sections, the replacement or introduction of new architectural elements. So many changes have contributed to the history of the cathedral complex, that it is difficult to follow it precisely. Even today there are many doubts concerning aspects of chronology or of attribution, which scholars still continue to research.

A general view of the Cathedral and surroundings.

History of the Piazza

The area of the Cathedral, Campanile and Baptistery is the heart, both in urbanistic and spiritual terms, of the whole city. For centuries sacred and profane performances and ceremonies have taken place in this piazza. The two most famous are the 'scoppio del carro' (explosion of the cart) at Easter, and the celebrations held for Saint John the Baptist, patron saint of the city. According to the biography of the Saint, he was the last of the prophets and the first of the apostles, and therefore of vital importance.

Saint John is, in fact, the link between the Old and New Testaments representing the person who administers baptism, the first of the Holy Sacraments, and therefore the first step towards salvation.
On the 24th of June, the day dedicated to the Patron Saint, public celebrations and rituals were held in the piazza in conjunction with the city's republican government. The image of the saint decorated the banner of the city council. Inside the Baptistery, the silver altar of Saint John was moved into the centre directly under the apex of the dome. The Baptistery was under the control of the most powerful guild, the Calimala, which represented all the merchants. During the three day celebration of Saint John a large market was held in the city, providing merchants, bankers and all others belonging to the guild, with an occasion to show off their wealth and power. On the afternoon of the most important day of festivities, the 24th, a race of

unsaddled horses was run from one side of the city to the other.
In terms of town planning, the piazza began to take on its present aspect from 1057 on, when the Regent of the Emperor Hohenstaufen moved to Florence. The decision to enlarge the Baptistery dates from then. The area was, however, crowded with buildings of all sorts, even including a cemetry. Only at the end of the 13th century, both as the result of a politically and economically positive period and in order to match the cities of Pisa and Siena which were building their religious monuments at this time, was it decided to enlarge the cathedral. In 1289 it was decided to completely re-pave the piazza and shortly after came the commission to plan a new cathedral in place of the existing one, which was entrusted to Arnolfo di Cambio.

The Baptistery

According to tradition, the Baptistery was built on a temple dedicated to Mars, which was later transformed into a church. For a long time this pagan origin remained a characteristic of the monument which, to Florentines of the 14th and 15th centuries, still represented the noble, Roman origins of the city.
The structure of the building dates back to about the 5th century. However it assumed its present form only after internal and external alterations made between the 11th and 13th centuries, in which marble materials from the Roman period were used, as they were abundantly available in the area around the piazza. Originally the Baptistery would certainly have been much smaller even compared to the ancient church of Saint Reparata and was probably enlarged in the 11th century by a sort of enclosure. With the economic and political expansion of Florence, it was decided to consolidate this enlargement by building a roof, and by having it consecrated in 1059 by Pope Nicholas II. The facing must have been entirely marble until then. In the middle of the 12th century as part of a project enlarging the building, the granite columns salvaged from another site, were put into place, and the attic storey under the dome was raised. In 1174 the lantern was built.
The choice of an octagonal form is not simply chance. We know that it corresponds to a precise religious symbology related to the new life offered in Christ. A source, probably to be found in Saint Ambrose, relates the number eight to baptism since it is through this that man may reach salvation, - the “octava dies”, in other words the eighth day after the seven, limited, earthly ones. The theme of salvation is therefore closely linked both to the sacrament of baptism and to the number eight. The building was used as a cathedral during the 11th century probably due to work on Saint Reparata, but then returned to its original function.

The Baptistery of San Giovanni

Exterior of the Baptistery

The baptistery is dressed with white and green marble from Prato. The sides are divided into three both vertically and horizontally. The lower level is divided by pilaster strips (on the blind sides) or by columns (on the sides with doors) which support an entablature around the entire circumference. The middle level is divided by semi-circular arches which rest on octagonal demi-pilasters and which enclose windows with alternately rounded or triangular pediments. A cornice underlies the third and last level, the attic, which has marble panels divided by grooved pilaster strips, added in the thirteenth century.
The dome, which is covered externally by an octagonal roof, rests on a small

decorated cornice, and culminates in the lantern (c. 1150).
The rectangular apse is dated 1202 and replaced an earlier semi-circular one. The coat of arms of the Calimala Guild (an eagle holding a bail in its claws) is engraved in the curved pediment of the central window, above Ghiberti's door on the northern side. During the Middle Ages numerous Roman sarcophagi, were placed around the Baptistery. They came from near-by Borgo San Lorenzo where important families of Roman times were buried. They are now in the Cathedral Museum.

The Baptistery Doors

The three Baptistery doors were made by different artists and at different times. Together they represent a piece of Florence's artistic history, demonstrating the move from the Gothic style of the 13th and 14th centuries, to that of international Gothic, and later the Renaissance. During the second World War the doors were removed, but were put back in 1948 after restoration. In 1966 however, they were damaged by the flood.
The original panels of the Door of Paradise are now in the Museo dell'Opera del Duomo.
The doors are decorated with groups of sculptures representing the life of St. John. They are all works of the 16th century, and replaced the earlier sculptures by Tino di Camaino, once placed within tricuspid tabernacles which no longer exist.
The iconographic theme of the decoration on the exterior, as well as that on the interior, is centered around the figure of Saint John the Baptist, the process of salvation, and the first sacrament in that process, baptism.

South Door

(Andrea Pisano, bronze casting by Leonardo d'Avanzo, a Venetian artisan called to Florence to undertake the work: 1330-1336).
The door was first placed on the side of the Baptistery facing the Cathedral in 1338, but was later moved from there to be replaced by Ghiberti's door (The Door of Paradise).
This is the only work signed by Andrea, and is dated on the frame 1330. The Calimala Guild, consisting of the city's merchants and the financial guardians of the Baptistery, decided in 1322 to replace the old wooden doors and commissioned the new bronze ones.
The first door to be made was that on the east side, facing the Cathedral. In artistic terms its immediate predecessors were the doors made by Bonanno in Pisa. They also provided a technical example since metal casting was not a common process in this area even though the process had remained unchanged since ancient times. The technique of casting with wax which

The South Door, designed by Andrea Pisano

was used for all three doors, involves making a wax model, which is then covered with a clay shell. This form is then baked and has channels for pouring in the melted metal. As the group is being baked, the wax melts, leaving a hollow which will then be filled by the melted metal. When the metal has later cooled, the shell is broken and the resulting sculpture is finished off with chasing and a graving tool. The reliefs were worked on separately by Andrea, a panel at a time. They were then chased and, after gilding, were positioned in the frame using a system of riveting around the edges (without screws). Venetian experts had to be summoned to do the work of casting, as there were no expert Florentine founders. The secrets of their art then became known, to the extent that even Ghiberti used them in making the Door of Paradise.

DESCRIPTION:
28 squares with Gothic quatrefoil, panels with scenes from the life of the Baptist in the twenty upper panels and '*Humility' and the 'Seven Theological and Cardinal Virtues'* in the last eight. These reliefs are slightly larger than the others, but they are also more crowded with figures. In the corners and along the sides of the squares there are twenty four decorative lions heads on each leaf, and a row of alternating rosettes and diamonds. The scenes are read like a book, from left to right and from top to bottom.

South Door, Andrea Pisano: the Baptism of Christ

(left leaf): *The Angel and Zacharias; Zacharias is struck dumb; The Visitation; The Birth of John the Baptist; The Naming of John the Baptist; John goes into the Wilderness; John preaches to the People; Behold the Lamb; John baptises the People; John baptises Christ; Hope; Faith; Fortitude; Temperance.*
(right leaf): *John before Herod; John is Imprisoned; John's disciples visit him in Prison; Christ Healing; Salome dances for Herod; The Beheading of John; The Head of John is brought to Herod; Salome brings Herodias the Head of John; John's Disciples remove his body; The Burial of John the Baptist; Charity, Humility; Justice; Prudence.*
The story follows the Gospels very

closely, interpreted also according to later sources on the life of the Saint. The iconography too is traditional, its immediate predecessors being the stories of the Baptist in the mosaics inside the Baptistery, and Giotto's cycle in the Peruzzi Chapel in Santa Croce. No sculpture existed to which direct reference could be made.
Andrea Pisano displayed both his ability as a goldsmith and his skill as a creative sculptor in the synthetic style used in relating the stories (both in the landscapes and in the buildings). The classical nature of the sharp division and clarity of the scenes distances the work from medieval sculptural style, characterized by an *horror vacui* - an antipathy to empty spaces. If the relationship between figures and background reminds us of the model found in Bonanno's work, the use of the varied quadrefoil shape recalls the Italian Gothic tradition. However, the episodes are summarized and described in a style which remained valid until Ghiberti's day.
It is worth noting that the most important scenes in the life of the Baptist are at eye-level, for example, the Baptism of Christ, with the apparant transparancy of the water on Christ's body. The Virtues, enthroned and with hexagonal halos, can all be identified by their symbols and by the Gothic writing at the bottom. The frame of the door is, instead, Renaissance (1452-62), the work of Vittorio Ghiberti, son of Lorenzo, and was made when the door was transferred from the east to the south side. Above the door is a bronze sculpture depicting the Baptist, Salome and the Executioner by Vincenzo Danti. This replaced a previous one by Tino di Camaino, of the Baptism of Christ, now lost.

South Door, Andrea Pisano: Charity

North Door

(Lorenzo Ghiberti, assisted by Masolino, Donatello, Michelozzo, Paolo Ucello) In 1401 the Calimala guild held a public competition to choose the artist who would make the second door. Brunelleschi and Jacopo della Quercia participated, but the commission was won by the panel presented by Ghiberti who from now on worked continuously on this and the third and last door, as well as on other commissions, almost all Florentine. The theme of the trial piece for the competition (now in the Bargello Museum, along with the Brunelleschi panel) was the sacrifice of Isaac. In fact the announcement of the competition had specified that the subject had to be taken from the Old Testament, but this was later modified to a choice of stories from the New Testament. The work was begun in 1403, and was put into place in 1424. The technique used was the same as that for the first door.

DESCRIPTION:
There are twenty eight squares, of which the upper twenty represent stories from the New Testament, and the remaining panels, the *Four Evangelists* and the *Four Doctors of the Church*. Here, the reading order of the stories runs from the bottom towards the top, according to northern tradition. The first series, the *Annunciation*, is in the third row from the bottom, and the last series, the *Pentecost*, is at the top on the right. After the Annunciation the story continues with the *Nativity* and the *Announcement to the Shepherds* (in a single panel), the *Adoration of the Magi, Christ among the Doctors, the Baptism of Christ by John, the Temptation in the Wilderness, the Expulsion of the Money-Changers from the Temple, Christ walks on the Water, the Transfiguration, the Raising of Lazarus, the Entry into Jerusalem, the Last Supper, the Agony in the Garden, the Betrayal of Judas, the Flagellation, Christ before Pilate, the Way to Calvary, the Crucifixion, the Resurrection, Pentecost.* The formal arrangement of the door is the same as that of Pisano's, except that the lion's heads which decorate the external frames of the panels have been replaced by portrait heads, among which there is the self portrait of Ghiberti. The composition of the scenes is quite different however, being quite animated and fluid, with frequent references to antiquity. Ghiberti uses many natural elements in the decoration of the frames - amongst the foliage, for example, one can see small animals such as a frog, a snail, or a salamander.
Above the door there is a bronze sculpture by Giovan Francesco Rustici of *Saint John the Baptist, the Levite and the Pharisee* (1506-11). It is stylistically similar to the work of Leonardo da Vinci, of whom Rustici was a pupil.

North Door, Lorenzo Ghiberti: The Annunciation. Facing page: the North Door

East Door (Gates of Paradise)

The door was so named by Michelangelo referring to the beauty of the work, but it is probably also a reference to the path of redemption, since this door is the entrance to the the place of baptism. It is the work of Lorenzo Ghiberti assisted by his sons, Tommaso and Vittorio, and by Michelozzo, Benozzo Gozzoli, Bernardo Cennini etc. This time the guild did not hold a competition, but gave a free hand to Ghiberti to carry out the work. In 1452 the door was placed in its present position, in place of Pisano's door. The various stages of its creation were as follows: commissioned the 2nd of January 1425; wax models completed in 1429;, bronze panels cast in 1437; completed in April 1452; gilding undertaken between April and June; finally, the decision to place it on the east side in July of the same year. The technical process of casting is similar to that of the other doors, at least as far as the structure of the two leaves is concerned. They were made in a single casting and are divided by twenty four medallions on the internal frames. The ten squares,fixed by pressure, contain ten reliefs illustrating stories from the Old Testament, and 48 small figures inside niches form the frame. The figures are of *Prophets, Sibyls*, and other biblical characters. Here too, as on the north door, we can see Ghiberti's self portrait (on the left-hand leaf, it is the third figure from the bottom). The original panels are in the Museo dell'Opera del Duomo.
This time Ghiberti changed completely the arrangement of the doors, choosing ten linear squares, which since they were larger, provided more space to recount the stories. He was thus able to include more than one episode in each panel lending a spatial complexity to the story which he managed with great expertise. He employed various techniques to obtain the effect of space and distance. In the first panel, containing the *Creation of Adam and Eve, Original Sin* and *Expulsion from Paradise*, three techniques can be seen: the varying depth of relief; the different proportions of the figures in the foreground and the background; the gradual reduction of detail.
The sequence of the stories continues, starting from the top left, with *Genesis*; *Cain and Abel*; *the murder of Abel*; *God and Cain*; in the third panel: *Noah's Sacrifice*; *the Drunkeness of Noah*. There are images of some exotic animals, such as the lion and the elephant, animals that were certainly not well known in the 15th century. In the panel portraying *the Apparition of the Angels to Abraham* and *the Sacrifice of Isaac*, Ghiberti returns to the subject of the famous original competition for the previous door. Here, however, priority is given to the appearance of the three angels to Abraham, an elegantly Gothic figure even in the sculptural strength of the

East Door (Gates of Paradise), by Lorenzo Ghiberti

relief. The next panel portrays (from left to right) *the Birth of Esau and Jacob; the Selling of the Firstborn; Rebecca advises Jacob; Rebecca speaks to God; Isaac orders Esau to go hunting; Esau goes hunting*. From the spatial point of view this is one of the most complex panels, together with the panel beside it. Both are framed by an architectural perspective which fully represent the theories of Brunelleschi. The two panels are at eye level, and stand out from the others because the two episodes take place in a monumental setting. The sixth panel representing *Joseph sold to the Merchants; the Discovery of the Gold Cup in Benjamin's Sack; Joseph is recognised by his Brothers*, is the central theme of the work. The decision to make the door in ten panels rather than twenty-four seems to date from around 1435, at the time of the return of Cosimo from exile and his return to power. The episode in the *Story of Joseph* which represents the discovery of Benjamin's cup and the distribution of the grain, ending in Joseph and Benjamin's embrace and forgiveness, has been seen as a reference to Cosimo's return to the city and the ensuing economic well-being which he brought, as well as forgiveness of those who had sent him into exile. The story continues with *Moses recieving the Law on Mount Sinai*, with a multitude of people representing the Hebrews. *The People of Israel in Jordan and the Taking of Jericho* shows Joshua leading the people of Israel to the Promised Land, and the battle of Jericho. The last two panels at the bottom take into account the position of the observer, that is, from above. These are the *Battle against the Philistines*, the *Killing of Goliath*, with the mythical biblical hero, David, defeating the giant Goliath (during the Renaissance, David often appears as a symbol of the city of Florence) and *Solomon receives the Queen of Sheba*. This last panel, which completes the series of stories, has in common with the two central panels, a background of architectural perspective. The three panels would

East Door (Gates of Paradise), Lorenzo Ghiberti: Joseph sold to the Merchants

East Door (Gates of Paradise), Lorenzo Ghiberti: the Work of the Forefathers

therefore seem to be connected in an important message, both political and religious. The return to power of Cosimo did not only benefit the city economically, but also helped to bring about the union between the Greek and Roman churches, ratified by the Council of Florence in 1439, and here symbolized by the meeting of the two representatives.

The technique, restoration and conservation of the work:

each sculpture is made in bronze cast on a wax model as described for the previous doors. It was then engraved and chased, and finally the whole surface was gilded using a technique in which the gold was dissolved in mercury which then evaporated in the heat of the furnace, leaving the gold fixed to the metal structure underneath.

East Door (Gates of Paradise), Lorenzo Ghiberti: Creation of Adam and Eve

From as early as 1475 onwards the door was subject to frequent washings, which were later stopped. The dirt which then accumulated was later painted over and thus formed a uniform layer, concealing the gilding. More restoration work, carried out in the eighteenth century worsened the situation. During the war the doors were removed and hidden outside Florence. They were then restored by the technicians of the Central Institute for Restoration. The Gates of Paradise had to be removed from their original position for reasons of conservation, - during the flood of 1966 six panels came away from the main structure. Since 1979, the panels have been systematically removed for scientific restoration and relocated in the

Museum, as has the rest of the door. Technical changes inherent in the process of combining certain metals, such as gold and copper, or gold and bronze, as well as damage caused by atmospheric factors (Piazza del Duomo is at the centre of a highly polluted area) are the causes of such deterioration. The dark patches on the panels of the Gates of Paradise are the signs of a clumsy attempt in the past to reveal the original gilding by scraping off the patina.

Above the door there was a marble sculpture of *Christ and John the Baptist* (1502) by Andrea Sansovino, completed by Vincenzo Danti, put in place in 1569, and an *Angel* (1791-92) by Innocenzo Spinazzi. This sculpture remained in place until August 1975, when a severe storm caused such damage to it that it had to be taken to the Opificio delle Pietre Dure for restoration, where it still is today. It will probably be replaced by a copy. The work is extremely important in Florentine 16th century sculpture. It was commissioned in 1502 from Sansovino, who prepared the overall design and who probably began with the figure of *Saint John*. Vincenzo Danti then finished the group with the figure of *Christ* (1566-67). To the sides of this façade are the two porphry columns which, according to tradition, were given to the Florentines by Pisa in gratitude for their help in the conquest of the Balearic Islands (about 1115). They could also have been booty from the same war.

East Door (Gates of Paradise), Lorenzo Ghiberti: Battle against the Philistines.

The Baptistery Interior

The interior of the Baptistery contains elements which recall its noble Roman origins, especially the use of marble enriched by typically Medieval decoration (mosaic). The floor is in tarsia with oriental style motifs. The walls are divided into three parts, on the lower level by monolithic columns in oriental granite taken from the ruins of other buildings, probably from a pagan temple in the Roman forum, alternated with grooved marble pilasters, and above by marble pilaster strips which enclose the double light windows of the women's gallery. The mosaics in the parapet of the women's gallery represent the prophets. The walls of the niches on the lower level

are clad in bichromatic marble in geometric designs, while the walls on the upper level are painted to imitate white and green marble.Some also have mosaics.
In the vaults behind the double lights of the women's gallery the decorations are either painted or in mosaic.
The segments of the dome rest on an attic storey consisting of squares, some containing images of saints in mosaic.
Little remains of the works of art made for and housed in the Baptistery as it has undergone considerable alteration.
In 1576-77 Bernardo Buontalenti removed the choir in front of the apse and dismantled the baptismal font which was in the centre of the building (as mentioned by Dante) for the christening of Filippo, son of Grand Duke Francesco I. Some remnants of the font can be seen in the entrance to the Museo dell'Opera del Duomo.
In 1731-32 Girolamo Ticciati replaced the altar with one in baroque style which in turn was removed in 1912 and is now in the courtyard of the same museum (the statues of *Saint John carried in Glory by Two Angels* and two candlesticks in the form of *Angels)*. Some fragments of the old choir enclosure are also in the museum entrance.
Donatello made the *Mary Magdalen* now in the Opera del Duomo for the Baptistery.
Entering the Baptistery, on both sides of the door are two *holy water stoups*.

On the right: *baptismal font* in marble with six reliefs referring to baptism (*John baptizes Christ, John baptizes the Crowd, Sylvester baptizes Constantine, a Priest baptizes the Young, Christ baptizes the Apostles, Christ baptizes John*) in the style of

Baptistery interior, apse

the Pisan school (1371).
On the floor: around the font, three rectangular panels, more decorated than the rest, with designs partly taken from oriental fabric designs; two other panels, one with the signs of the zodiac, are in front of the Door of Paradise.
On the next wall: *tomb of the Antipope John XXIII* (Cardinal Baldassare Coscia, who died in Florence in 1419). Commissioned in 1421 by his heirs, it has a gilded bronze statue by Donatello who probably modelled the image of

Baptistery interior, women's gallery

the Cardinal on a death mask, and niches with the *three Theological Virtues* (1421-27) by Michelozzo. Michelozzo is also responsible for the *Madonna and Child* above the tomb. The two artists collaborated on the overall design, which is the earliest example of a Renaissance tomb. There is some disagreement concerning the attribution of various parts to the two artists: the relief of the Virtues has also been attributed to Donatello on stylistic grounds, and opinion also differs regarding the dating of the work. The effect of illusion, created by the curtain held above by a ring and falling like real material should be noted. The effect must have been even greater originally when the marble was coloured.

The *Sarcophagus of Bishop Ranieri*: (Bishop of Florence 1071-1113) with a fine tomb slab in green and white marble.

Apse or Tribune (1202): probably the first area to be decorated was the vault, supported by four Roman columns and decorated by Byzantine style mosaics, the work of the Franciscan monk, Jacob, whose signature can be read "fratris Francisci frater". He was active before the death of Saint Francis (before 1226). The mosaics depict a large wheel held up by four profane images of *Atlas*, kneeling on Corinthian capitals. The wheel encircles the figure of the *Agnus Dei* (the Holy Lamb) in the centre, surrounded by *Prophets* and *Patriarchs* and a decoration of vases,

doves, heads and angels. On each side of the wheel there is a figure: the *Virgin "teotòkos"* holding the Christ child raising his hand in blessing and Saint John the Baptist enthroned. The detail of the central wheel is not simply an abstract decoration, but has a specific iconographic significance. It has been interpreted as the 'celestial sphere', a symbol of ancient origin (an earlier example is also found in one of the domes of San Marco in Venice) which referred to cosmology , but which in Christianity, assumes a different meaning, that of the *Heavenly City* - the city of God. The symbolism of the circle is often closely

Michelozzo and Donatello, Tomb of the Antipope, John XXIII

Baptistery, mosaic decoration in the apse

Baptistery, detail of the mosaic decoration in the apse

linked to the earlier iconography of the sun with the signs of the zodiac around its rays, similar to that in the apse. (An iconographical interpretation is given later, with reference to the mosaics in the dome).

The double arch at the front of the apse: on either side at the bottom of the upper arch there are two nude figures on wild beasts from which a floral decoration of vines begins, ending at the top of the arch, in a figure of *Christ*. The lower arch has figures of the *Apostles* and *Evangelists* with that of *John the Baptist* in the centre. The intrados of the arch has images of the *prophets* inside small niches and in the centre a medallion with the *Virgin*. Probably the motifs are not entirely decorative, but symbolic. The wild beasts represent Evil which threatens mankind, who, in fleeing from it clings to his faith in God as symbolised by the vines traditionally indicating the Tree of Life.

The Altar: this was reconstructed in 1914 with original fifteenth century pieces, which had been saved when dismanteled in 1731. The marble angel candelstick to the right of the altar is by Agostino di Jacopo (1320). The angel is on a decorated column, in its turn resting on a stylobate lion.

The floor: consisting of 13th century *tarsia squares* with gratings which give light to the level underground, where there is a black and white Roman floor in 'opus tessellatum' with geometric designs, discovered in 1912-15.

Baptistery, detail of the mosaic decoration in the apse

On the next wall there is the Roman *sarcophagus* of Giovanni da Velletri, Bishop of Florence (died 1230); a statue of *John the Baptist* by Giuseppe Piamontini (1688); a Roman *sarcophagus* with a design of a wild boar hunt, and the coats of arms of the Medici family and the Wool Guild, in memory of Guccio de' Medici, standard-bearer in 1299, who was buried there.

Baptistery Interior: The Dome

The dome was begun at the top by Fra' Jacopo, or by his workshop and then continued by artists of the Venetian byzantine school (in Florence the tradition of mosaic work was fairly limited). The artists also worked from cartoons provided by Tuscan artists such as Meliore, 'Maestro della Maddalena' (*the Story of Saint John, the Adoration of the Magi, the Journey of the Magi, the Flight to Egypt*), Coppo di Marcovaldo (*Christ in Judgement* and *the Universal Judgement*), and Cimabue (the *first story of John*, and two *stories of Joseph*). Work on the decoration was already well advanced in 1271 and it was still being worked on in 1300. It therefore provides a panorama of different styles, both in geographical and chronological terms, ranging from the late Bizantine and Romanesque tradition up to an early Giotto style. The mosaics were restored by Baldinovetti (1481-90) and again between 1898 and 1907 with additions

Michelozzo: one of the three Theological Virtues, detail of the Tomb of the Antipope John XXIII

Donatello: Mary Magdalene, now in the Museo dell'Opera del Duomo, originally in the Baptistery

to complete some scenes.
Iconographically the dome is divided into circles and segments: on the upper level, around the lantern there are symbolic designs of plants (fronds of vines, deer at water, peacocks) and figures holding shields in Early Christain style. On the level immediately below, starting from the side of the apse, we see *Christ between two seraphs* and the heavenly heirarchy (*Thrones*, *Dominations*, *Angels*, *Archangels*, *Cherubims*, *Principalities*, *Virtues*). On the three lower levels, in the three sections near the apse are *Christ in Judgement* and, to the sides, on the upper level, Angels with theTrumpets of Judgement and the *Symbols of the Passion*. On the middle level the *Virgin* is on the left, *Saint John the Baptist* on the right, and the *Apostles enthroned* in the foreground with angels in the background. Finally on the lowest level there are *three Patiarchs* on the left, and the *Universal Judgement* with the Chosen and the Damned. The scene of the *Universal Judgement* begins at the feet of the immense figure of *Christ in Judgement* (eight metres high), with the group of the Chosen on the left and a detail of *Hell* on the right. In the first group there are symbolic figures from lay and ecclesiastic society: sovreigns; Friars from the most important orders (Dominican and Franciscan); Bishops and ordinary citizens, all of which are a summary of the society of the time

Coppo di Marcovaldo, Universal Judgement (detail)

Baptiatery, the mosaics in the vault

which consisted of civil power (nobility), the religious classes (secular and regular orders) with their various heirarchical representatives, and the ordinary citizen (it should be remembered that the Baptistery was under the protection of the merchants' guild).
On the other side, to the right of *Christ* there is the group of the Damned. Here there are allusions to heretics, who are difficult to identify, as well as allegories of sin portrayed with traditional symbolism, concluding with

Baptistery, the mosaics in the vault (detail)

a terrifying panorama, including on the bottom right the image of Jude, symbol of betrayal, hanged. In the remaining five sections, reading from left to right (each scene is separated from the others by a column and there are three scenes in each section) we see:

first circle, *Genesis*
second circle: *Story of Joseph*
third circle: *Story of Christ* (from the Annunciation to the Resurrection)
fourth circle: *Story of John the Baptist.*
The order starts with the section to the right of the *Angels*, *Apostles* and *Hell*,

Baptistery, the mosaics in the vault: Christ in Judgement

Baptistery, the mosaics in the vault, first section

running from the upper level to the lower level.

GENESIS

There are fourteen panels, one less than the other circles because the penultimate episode of the animals entering the Ark occupies two panels.
1. *The Creation* with the *Almighty* in a circle of stars in the act of creation and, beneath, in the presence of the *Sun* and the *Moon*, there is a description of terresrial nature with the sea, mountains and animals. The two figures, one male and one female, observing the scene, could perhaps be interpreted as the personifications of the *Sun* (male) and of the *Moon* (female), as the colours used

Baptistery, the mosaics in the vault, first section, Genesis

Baptistery, the mosaics in the vault, first section: the Story of Joseph

Baptistery, the mosaics in the vault, second section

correspond to those of the two planets.
2. *The Creation of Adam*
3. *The Creation of Eve from Adam's Rib*
4. *Original Sin*
5. *The Rebuke*
6. *The Banishment from Paradise*, in which *Adam* is portrayed with a farm implement (representing male work) and *Eve* with a spindle (female work).
7. *The Work of the Forefathers*
8. *The Sacrifice of Cain and Abel*
9. *Cain kills Abel*
10, 11, 12. The next three panels are modern reconstructions. They are signed and dated 1906.
13, 14. *The Animals entering the Ark*
15. *The Flood.*

The Story of Joseph

The Story of Joseph has a prophetic

Baptistery, the mosaics in the vault, second section: Story of Christ

Baptistery, the mosaics in the vault, second section: Genesis

Baptistery, the mosaics in the vault, third section

implication, anticipating the story of *Christ* and, chronologically, is close to the stories on the upper level of *Adam and Eve, Cain and Abel, Noah.*

1. *Joseph's dream*
2. *Relating the Dream to the Parents,* with the group of the brothers on one side, and the mother and father on the other beneath a canopy
3. *Joseph and his Brothers*
4. *Joseph is sold to the Merchants*
5. *The Brothers bring the False News of Joseph's Death to the Parents*
6. *Joseph's Journey*
7. *The Presentation to Potiphar*
8. *Joseph is taken to Prison by Potiphar and his Wife*
9. *Joseph in Prison*

Baptistery, the mosaics in the vault, fourth section: Story of Christ

Baptistery, the mosaics in the vault, fourth section: Story of Christ

Baptistery, the mosaics in the vault, second section: Story of Christ

Baptistery, the mosaics in the vault, first section: Story of Christ

10. *The Pharaoh's Dream*
11. *Interpretation of the Pharaoh's Dream*
12. *Joseph is made Viceroy of Egypt*
13. *The Store of Grain*
14. *The Pardoning of the Brothers*
15. *Meeting with his Father*

THE STORY OF CHRIST

1. *The Annunciation*
2. *The Visitation*
3. *The Nativity*
4. *Adoration of the Magi*
5. *The Dream of the Magi*
6. *Return of the Magi*
7. *The Presentation at the Temple*
8. *An Angel suggests Flight to Joseph*
9. *The Flight into Egypt*
10. *The Slaughter of the Innocents*
11. *The Last Supper*
12. *The Kiss of Judas*
13. *The Crucifixtion*
14. *The Deposition*
15. *The Resurrection*

THE STORY OF SAINT JOHN
(corresponding to fifteen of the twenty stories on Pisano's door)

1. *The Annunciation of the Angel to Zacharias*
2. *The Birth of Saint John*
3. *Saint John in the Desert*
4. *The Sermon of Saint John*
5. *The Prophecy of the Coming of the Saviour*
7. *The Baptism of Christ*
8. *John before Herod*
9. *John in Prison*

Baptistery, the mosaics in the vault, fifth section: Story of San Giovanni

Baptistery, the mosaics in the vault, fourth section

10. *The Message to the Two Disciples*
11. *The Miracle of Christ in the presence of the Disciples*
12. *Herod's Feast*
13. *The Beheading*
14. *The Presentation of the Baptist's Head*
15. *The Burial*

The stories of Saint John the Baptist are those nearest to the faithful, according to the concept that the Patron Saint is an intermediary between the believer and his faith. The similarity between some of the stories of *John* and of *Christ* can, in fact, be seen. The sentencing to death of John is placed underneath the *Crucifixion*, and the *Burial of John* is under the empty tomb of Christ on the day of Resurrection. This is to emphasise the value of human sacrifice for faith. Clearly the aim is didactic, we return

Baptistery, the mosaics in the vault, fifth section

to the idea of a Bible for the poor, so that those who could not read could learn the precepts of the Church from the pictures. The message given in the mosaics is therefore that of the return to Christ and of ultimate salvation through prayer and the sacraments, beginning with baptism, as well as a warning against sin (in the terrifying images of Hell).
It is worth mentioning an interesting theory concerning the overall iconography of the mosaics: it has been suggested that a single plan of both a cosmological and biblical nature was behind the symbolism in the various parts of the Baptistery. The scene of the Apocalypse is immediately above the entrance to the apse; in the Apocalypse according to Saint John there is a passage describing *Heavenly Jerusalem* (the City of God) which

Baptistery, the mosaics in the vault, fourth section: Genesis

contains all the elements found here in the decoration of the apse: Jerusalem illuminated by the golden rays radiating from the Glory of God (coinciding with the *Sacred Lamb* in the centre of the circle like the sun). The four kneeling male figures on the capitals in the corners of the vault could represent the four elements (air, water, earth and fire) or perhaps the four rivers of Paradise. The presence of *Saint John the Baptist Enthroned* is due to the specific purpose of the monument. The meaning could correspond to that of the images in the dome, where man approaches salvation first and foremost through the sacrament of baptism. As regards the floor, we can see that the inscribed shapes of the square and the circle are repeated here. This is not only by chance since, according to medieval thought, the square indicates finite time, and the circle indicates the perfection of the heavenly sphere, and the infinite. The relationship between the square and the circle would therefore be a reference to the notion of continuity between the two spheres. One of the slabs in the flooring also refers to the heavenly sphere. It is no longer in its original position (which was probably in the centre, corresponding to the apex of the dome), but is now in front of the east door and represents the circle of the zodiac with its twelve symbols around the rays of the sun.

Baptistery, the mosaics in the vault, second section: Story of San Giovanni

Baptistery, the mosaics in the vault, first section: Story of Christ

Baptistery, the mosaics in the vault, panel on the left of Christ in Judgement

THE CATHEDRAL

The Cathedral is the fourth largest church in the world, after Saint Peter's in Rome, Saint Paul's in London and Milan Cathedral.
It was built in various phases:
- 1296, building began under Arnolfo di Cambio to replace the old cathedral of Saint Reparata, which continued to be called such until the beginning of the 15th century. Arnolfo built the façade and the sides, beginning with the one on the right as one looks at the building, according to a plan which will be explained in more detail later. After his death (1302), worked continued more slowly;

Baptistery, the mosaics in the vault, panel to the right of Christ in Judgement

-1331, responsibility for the construction was given to the Authorities of the 'Opera', an institution created specifically to supervise work on the new cathedral, which was financed by the Wool Guild (whose emblem of the *Holy Lamb* is often found throughout the decoration;the emblem of the Opera is instead the inscription OPA, the P standing for PER);
- 1334-37: Giotto was the master builder, and dedicated himself almost entirely to the Campanile;
-1357-64: work was directed by Francesco Talenti and Giovanni di Lapo Ghini, who enlarged the original project; during this phase it was decided to build the dome, and the

Detail of the mosaics in the apse

Detail of the mosaics in the apse

citizens of Florence were asked to express their opinion regarding this change;
- 1367: a second public competition was held in which the opinion of the citizens was consulted. The project presented by four artists and four architects won. Together they formed a real team of experts, consisting of goldsmiths, painters and stone cutters who worked for the Silk and Spice Guild. Andrea Orcagna, Taddeo Gaddi and Andrea di Bonaiuto were among the artists;
- 1378: the vault of the middle nave was completed;
- 1380-1421 the tribunes and the drum of the dome were built;
- 1434-36: Brunelleschi finshed the dome according to the plan with which he won the competition in 1418;
- 1445-1461: the lantern and bronze ball were finished.

The cathedral was consecrated in 1436 on the 25th of March by Pope Eugenius IV.

View of the Cathedral and the Campanile, south side

Detail of the nineteenth century façade

Cathedral - Exterior

The building is dressed with white marble from Carrara, green from Prato and pink from the Maremma. The different styles used illustrate the various chronological stages in its construction. For example there is a Romanesque flavour on the sides and the lower outer sides of the tribunes which have blind, rounded arches; the doors and the elegant double light windows are ogival and therefore Gothic in appearance. The dome is Renaissance, and lastly, although disguised as Gothic, the façade is nineteenth century.

Cathedral - Exterior - Façade

The old fourteenth century façade, designed by Arnolfo di Cambio, but never finished, was demolished in 1587. Arnolfo's plan for the façade was very 'classic', based on harmony and a sense of measure. The iconographical theme, which Arnolfo's statues now in the Museo dell'Opera del Duomo celebrated, was that of *Mary* (the name 'Santa Maria del Fiore' combines the dedication to the *Madonna* with that of the city of Florence). Statues for the façade were also made by Nanni di Banco, Donatello, Niccolò Lamberti and Bernardo Ciuffagni. The sculptures would have stood out against the colours of the white, green and red marble. Once Arnolfo had died, his successors (Giotto and Andrea Pisano) dedicated themselves to the Campanile.

Nor did Francesco Talenti change Arnolfo's plan. Until the 15th century, various sculptors continued to enrich the façade with statues. But by the end of the 15th century the façade no longer reflected the taste of the times and the proposal of building a completely new one began to be considered seriously. However it was only decided finally in 1587, when Grand Duke Francesco I ordered its demolition under the direction of Bernardo Buontalenti, carried out by the builder Zanobi di Graziadio. The work took five months and cost 250 'fiorini', as documents of the day tell us. However, Francesco died the following year and the façade remained unfinished for a long time.

When work began on the present Neo-gothic façade a faint trace of the 17th century fresco by Ercole Graziani could still be seen on the front of the building. This had been part of the decoration for the wedding of Prince Ferdinand and Violante di Baviera.

The present façade was built between 1871-1887, to a design by the Florentine architect Emilio De Fabris but the choice of medieval style was based on the preference for 'romanticism', popular in the preceding decades.

Before a final decision on how the cathedral should look, two competitions were held and much argument ensued between the two opposing parties, one supporting a 'basilica' style and the other a 'tricuspid' style. The

The Cathedral; the Baptistery and the Campanile

former preferred a horizontal design, as in fact was finally agreed, while the latter were fanatics of the Neo-gothic style, with its pointed lines and decorated with pinnacles and spires. The decorative plan was conceived by the historian and intellectual Augusto Conti, and has as its theme the grandeur of *Christianity* and the image of *Mary*, returning therefore to the original theme. The three bronze doors are the work of Andrea Passaglia (1897 the central door, 1903 the one on the left) and of Giuseppe Cassioli (1899 on the right).
The mosaics in the lunettes above the doors are a design of Niccolò Barabino. In the four tabernacles between the pilasters dividing the façade into three are statues of *Cardinal P. Valeriani, Bishop A. Tinacci, Saint Anthony,* and *Eugenius IV*, all of whom consecrated various parts of the cathedral. In the cusp above the central door is *Mary in Glory*, a relief by Augusto Passaglia. In the band beneath the rose window are tabernacles with statues of the *Madonna* and *Apostles*. Around and above the rose window are *busts of famous Florentines*. These statues are the work of some of the best Florentine sculptors of the day: Salvino Salvini, Tito Sarrocchi, Ulisse Cambi, Vincenzo Consani, Antonio Bortone, Amalia Dupré.
The façade of the cathedral can therefore be considered from two points of view: both as an architectural and sculptural work in itself and as a critical record of Florentine art in the last century.
Our visit continues on the right, with the Campanile.

CAMPANILE

General Structure

The campanile was designed by Giotto who worked on it from July 1334 until 1337, the year of his death. The artist planned the structure, a robust square tower with corner columns, but he only succeeded in building as far as the first cornice with the hexagonal tiles. His successsor was Andrea Pisano, master builder from 1337-47. He continued Giotto's design on the second storey, decorated by losange-shaped tiles, but then changed the design, dividing the four sides with two pilaster strips and introducing the element of Gothic niches (for statues) on the lower level and false niches above. Andrea Pisano left the work in 1348 and it was taken over by Francesco Talenti who completed it between 1350-59. Under his direction the Campanile took on a much lighter aspect with the introduction of pairs of Gothic double light windows. These openings, with their slender points and fine twisted columns lent an airy aspect to the building which then closed with the last, impressive storey of three-light windows, also pointed, - the conclusive touch to the building. The Campanile is then crowned by a projecting gallery supported by corbels and trefoil arches, and finished by an openwork railing, which lend a calm elegance to

the monument. The Campanile combines an overall respect for the Gothic style, with the impressive rigour of its rectilinear structure, in a way which is stylistically balanced and harmonised by the colour of the marbles (green, white from Carrara, and pink from the Maremma).
The present entrance door consists of an alteration made in 1431 when the original communicating passage between the Campanile and the Cathedral at the level of the first storey and used by the clerics, was removed. The last five hexagonal tiles, where the corridor was, were made by Luca della Robbia.
The stairs which climb to the top are a double spiralled ramp in the walls.

The Sculptures

The tiles which decorated the Campanile were all transferred to the Museo dell'Opera del Duomo for conservation in 1965 and 1967. Casts have been put in the place of the originals. The entire iconographic plan of the decoration (reliefs and statues) is based on the theme of the *Salvation of Mankind*. This was common in medieval iconography (often found in relief sculptures on church façades) and widespread in Scolastic philosophy. The evolutionary process is illustrated by human labour (which according to Scolastica was divided into Necessitas, Virtus and Sapientia), and by the *Cardinal and Theological Virtues*, by the sacraments of

The Campanile

Detail of the Campanile

Christian life, and by the images of those who in ancient times had announced the redemption, - *Kings, Sybils, Prophets* and *Patriarchs*.
The works should be read starting from the west side, continuing progressively to the south, east and north sides.
On the lower level:
hexagonal, marble tiles in bas-relief, by Andrea Pisano and workshop during the fourth to fifth decade of the 14th century. The last tiles are by Luca della Robbia.
Pisano's sculptures for the Campanile were his second great cycle of work for Florence. It is possible that he worked with Giotto from 1334 on, when Giotto was supervisor of work on the Campanile and Andrea was still

Detail of the Campanile

working on the Baptistery door. The spatial economy and sculptural strength of the tiles reflect the influence of the great painter. Iconography: from the *Creation to the Civilization of Man* by his skills or the 'mechanical crafts' (Necessitas) among which are included the figurative arts, as these were then considered equal to manual labour. There are also some figures recognised as being the instigators of social endeavour (Virtus).

The first seven hexagons (on the west side) relate the stories of Genesis: *Creation of Man, Creation of Woman, The Work of the Forefathers, Jabal* (farming), *Jubal* (music), *Tubalcain*

Andrea Pisano: two tiles from the Campanile, in the Museo dell'Opera del Duomo

(metalwork) and *Noah* (the grape harvest);
on the south side, *Jonitus* (astronomy), the *Art of Building*, *Medicine*, *Hunting*, *Wool making* (textiles), *Phroneus* (law), *Dedalus*;
on the east side (entrance side): *Navigation*, *Hercules* and *Cacus* (liberation of the Earth from monsters, or social justice), *Agriculture* (Homogirus), *Drama*, *Architecture*;
on the north side: *Phidias* (sculpture), *Apelle* (painting).
On the northern side, in place of the passage to the Cathedral, Luca della Robbia made the last five hexagons of the series begun by Andrea Pisano (1437-39).
The subjects are (from the liberal arts): *Grammar* (Donatus and pupils), *Dialectic* (with two philosophers, possibly Plato and Aristotle), *Rhetoric* or *Poetry* (Orpheus), *Arithmetic* (Euclides and possibly Pythagorus), *Geometry* or *Astrology* (Pythagorus or Tubalcain).
On the upper level:
rhomboid bas-relief tiles, with a blue majolica background, by Andrea Pisano and workshop, and seven tiles attributed to Maso di Banco.
If the first row of hexagonal tiles referred to human labour, within the theme of evolution, the second row refers to superhuman powers: these are the planets which, together with *Virtue* and the *Liberal Arts*, represent the natural, moral and spiritual forces on which man relies.
west side: *Saturn* (with the wheel of

Andrea Pisano: Prophet, in the Museo dell'Opera del Duomo

Donatello: Jeremiah, in the Museo dell'Opera del Duomo

Donatello: Beardless Prophet, in the Museo dell'Opera del Duomo

Donatello: Abacuc, in the Museo dell'Opera del Duomo

time), *Jupiter* (with the symbols of the Christian faith), *Mars* (an armed cavalier), the *Sun* or *Apollo* (with a sceptre), *Venus* (with two small admirers), *Mercury*, the *Moon*;
south side: *Faith* (goblet and crucifix), *Charity* (cornucopia), *Hope* (winged), *Prudence* (two faces), *Justice* (sword and scales), *Temperance* (pouring water), *Strength* (shield);
east side: *Astronomy*, *Music*, *Geometry*, *Grammar*, *Rhetoric*, *Logic*, *Arithmetic*;
north side: (the seven sacraments) *Baptism*, *Confession*, *Marriage*, *Priesthood*, *Confirmation*, *Eucarist*, *Extreme Unction*.

On the third level:
four niches on each side, with sixteen statues of *Prophets*, *Sybils and John the Baptist* (all copies, the originals are in the Museo dell'Opera del Duomo). For the west side Andrea Pisano had made the *Kings* and *Sybils* (1342-43), the last step in the process of salvation (1342-43). These statues were transferred to the north side and replaced by those which Donatello made between 1416 and 1436, the most important of these being *Abacuc* (referred to as the 'dunce'), *Jeremiah*, the *Beardless Prophet* (1415-18) the *Bearded Prophet* (1418-20) and *Abraham the Patriarch* sacrificing

Isaac, (1421) which he worked on with Nanni di Bartolo who is also probably the author of the *Bearded Prophet*.
The originals remained in place on the north and south sides until the second World War. *King David*, *King Solomon*, *the Eritrean Sybil*, the *Tiburtine Sybil*, and *Four Statues of Prophets*, are all the work of Andrea Pisano.
The entrance, with a relief of the *Lamb of God*, is on the east side of the Campanile.

Cathedral, the Campanile Door

Cathedral - Exterior - Right Side (south)

The oldest part of the building and of the 14th century decoration, are found on the right side, in the area beside the Campanile: a relief of the *Annunciation*, under which we can see the date 1310, attributed to a Tuscan artist (to the right of the entrance door to the Campanile); next is the *Campanile door* (door to the west of the south side). This is pointed and decorated with coloured marble, (the

Part of the southern tribune

sculptures are not at present in place); in the lunette: *Madonna and Child*, earlier attributed to the school of Andrea Pisano, and later to Simone Talenti (in the group of angels on the Cornacchini door); in the pediment, inside a tondo, *Christ Blessing*, earlier attributed to the school of Pisano, and later to Luca di Giovanni da Siena; on the lateral pinnacles: statues of *Gabriel* and *Our Lady of the Annunciation*, previously attributed to Niccolò Spinelli and other artists, but they were later entrusted to two different artists from different backgrounds and training; they have recently been attributed to Luca di Giovanni da Siena (*the Angel*) and to a pupil of Giovanni di Balduccio (*the Virgin*).
The following door - the *Door of the Canons*- (the door to the east of the south side), was sculpted and decorated by Lorenzo di Giovanni di Ambrogio and Piero di Giovanni Tedesco (as was the other door, called the 'Porta della Mandorla'), who completed it in 1378; in 1380 it was altered by Giovanni Fetti. In the lunette: *Madonna with Child*, by Niccolò di Pietro Lamberti (1395-96) and two *angels*, attributed to Lamberti or Lorenzo di Giovanni d'Ambrogio (c. 1402). In the apex: a tondo of *Christ with Angels* and above, a statue of the *Archangel Michael* (1377) by Zanobi di Bartolo; to the sides of the apex, two statues of *Prophets*, also attributed to Zanobi di Bartolo (1377).

Cathedral - Exterior - Apse

The apse of the cathedral is formed by three large linked tribunes with Gothic double lights on two levels and three small domes which echo the dome itself. The tribunes are reinforced by three straight butresses. Around the drum of the dome are four recesses in classical style, designed by Brunelleschi about 1440 as a purely decorative feature. Round the drum there are eight roundel windows. The gallery, constructed between 1506 and 1515 by Bacio d'Agnolo, criticised by Michelangelo as looking like a "cage for crickets", is on one side only (south east).

Cathedral - Exterior - Dome

"...a structure so enormous, as high as the heavens, big enough to cover all the people of Tuscany with its shadow". Thus Leon Battista Alberti spoke of Brunelleschi's work, revealing that the dome was perceived as being not just an architectural object, but as a 'spatial structure', a form which represented the entire universe. The term used by Alberti indicates an element which is in itself structural and self-supporting, and which has assimilated elements whose function in Gothic architecture was only partially that of support, making them instead, a part of the whole. The ribs of Brunelleschi's dome provide perspective, they converge in a point which is representative of infinity, so

The southern tribune

that the entire dome is a representation of the universe.
This feeling of spaciousness on high is emphasized by the fact that the dome is separated from the building below by the drum thus lending an autonomy to the roofing.
It is probable that the idea of building a dome dates from after 1357 during Francesco Talenti's period as director of works. Assisted by Giovanni di Lapo Ghini, he devised the octagonal drum. Talenti's design, later enlarged in the project of the artists and master-builders, contains in embryonic form the architectural solution arrived at by Brunelleschi.
The wide, irregular octagon (four sides are shorter, and four longer) formed where the naves meet the transept, is covered by an immense acute angled dome. The diameter above the drum is 45.52 metres; height, excluding the lantern, 91 metres). The dome is an amazing architectural machine, based on technology which was avant-garde for the times. The innovation lay in the fact that no reinforcement was used, as it would have been too large. No wood scaffolding would have been strong enough to bear the weight of the vault. Firstly the problem was resolved with the ingenious idea of a double frame, with a hollow between. The internal spherical vault (more than two metres thick) has a mainly structural function, and is self-supporting, based on the perfect arrangement of the quoins, while the outer sphere is the covering. Between these two vaults the system of stairs climbs to the summit. The two vaults are linked to each other by spurs, that is, the corner ribs, which are also visible on the outside, outlined in white marble on the red tiles, and by other vertical ribbing. Horizontally there are small linking arches between one spur and another. The outer openings in the dome light the staircase in the space between the two vaults, while those on the inner vault serve for ventilation. The dome was finished in 1434 and was blessed in August 1436.
Crowning the dome is the lantern, twenty metres high. It is covered by a cone supported on an octagonal base with eight radial butresses. On each of the eight sides there is an elongated, pointed opening framed by two half-columns with capitals of acanthus leaves.
We can see the same style in the Tower of the Winds, Athens, a small octagonal marble building of the first century B.C., and the Tribune of the Uffizi, with the lantern and rose window 'of the winds' - an earlier example of the octagonal plan. The relationship with the element of the wind is symbolic in nature and is reinforced by the fact that the lantern has an extremely important position, - the highest point on the most important building of the city.
The lantern had already been planned in Brunelleschi's original project of 1418. Once the serraglio (the keystone of the vault) on the dome had been completed in 1434, there remained the

The apse and dome

problem of the shape it should have. From March 1436 on, six models were produced by competing designers for the crowning structure, - Brunelleschi, Ghiberti, Antonio Manetti Ciaccheri and others - and once again Brunelleschi won.
In the later stages of its construction, which took 35 years, and went on long after the death of Brunelleschi, it was subject to various alterations which modified the original design. This, however, had never been completely defined by Brunelleschi partly due to professional secrecy.
Between 1436 and 1446, the year of his death, Brunelleschi concentrated mainly on the lantern. The first slabs of

A section of Brunelleschi's dome

The dome and apse of the cathedral

marble arrived in Florence, via the Arno, in 1443, and in March 1446 work was begun at the level of the serraglio. After Brunelleschi's death, Michelozzo became masterbuilder, followed by Antonio Manetti Ciaccheri until 1460. He, in turn was followed by Bernardo Rossellino and finally by Verrocchio. The commission for the bronze sphere was given to Verrocchio in 1468, and it was placed on the lantern in 1471. In 1601 it was hit by lightning and was completely rebuilt.
The lantern should be considered a gem of engraving on a massive scale, reflecting the close relationship between architecture and the applied arts, such as goldsmithing, engraving etc., which architects had also to study during their apprenticeship.

Cathedral - Exterior - Left side

The '*Porta della Mandorla*' (door to the east on the north side):
records tell us that the decoration was completed as far as the beginning of the arch in 1397 (the jambs and architrave), and that it is the work of several artists. Giovanni d'Ambrogio and Piero di Giovanni Tedesco were paid for the lower part in 1395.
Lorenzo di Giovanni d'Ambrogio made the two small statues of *Prophets* in the tabernacles in the lateral pilasters (1396-97). From 1391 Jacopo di Piero Guidi and Niccolò Lamberti worked on the door. The profiles of ten *angels* in the hexagons of the splayed jambs are in fact the work of four different artists.
The work was then interrupted until, in December of 1404, a council of the builders gave permission to Antonio di Banco and his son Nanni to work on the decoration of the arch. They, together with Lamberti, made the *Angels* in the arch of the doorway. The stylistic difference is visible in the traces of the antique style, a decidedly Early Renaissance trait, and in the decoration of the splayed door jambs which is unlike the late Gothic style.
The 'Porta della Mandorla' is a 'subsite' where, more than any other, we can see the change from traditional design to a newer one.
Once the decoration of the door had been completed, the lunette remained empty, until in 1409 the masterbuilders decided to place two figures from the *Annunciation* there. The figures (attributed to Jacopo della Quercia) were taken from the Altar of the Holy Trinity inside the church, and were placed here in 1414, on a blue painted background (now in the Museo dell'Opera del Duomo). The *Annunciation* is a theme which is perfectly in keeping with the iconography of the upper relief (on the Mandorla door) of the *Assumption of the Virgin Handing the Belt to Saint Thomas*. The hands of the *Virgin*, outstretched to *Saint Thomas*, are now empty, though originally they held a belt in silk edged in gold which was replaced in 1435 with one in copper.
From 1414 to 1421, the year of his

A detail of the 'Porta della Mandorla' with a relief by Nanni di Banco

death, Nanni di Banco worked on the relief which was put in place in 1422 by Battista d'Antonio.
In order to complete the door Bernardo Ciuffagni was given the task of sculpting a figure of *Santo Stefano* in the apex. Instead a statue of a *Prophet* by Piero di Giovanni Tedesco, which had not been used elsewhere, was put here.
On the pinnacles to the sides of the door there was a pair of *Prophets* in marble (now in the Museo dell'Opera del Duomo) believed to be a youthful work of Donatello, due to documents which mention two statues of *Prophets* made by him in 1408. They are two small statues in Gothic style which critics now attribute to different artists: the *small Prophet* on the left is attributed to Bernardo Ciuffagni, and the one on the right may be a youthful work of Luca della Robbia. Probably the two statues referred to in the Donatello documents are those now in the Opera del Duomo which were on the door of the Campanile.
The marble reliefs which complete the *Assumption* with a *Prophet* and a *Sybil* are by Donatello, for which he

received a payment of six 'fiorini' in 1422. The *Prophet* is taken from Roman examples of Barbarians and the Greek profile of the *Sybil* is also found in other feminine portraits by Donatello.
In 1489 the Cathedral Authorities and Builders decided to substite the sculpture in the lunette with a mosaic and commissioned Davide and Domenico Ghirlandaio. Dated 1490, the mosaic repeated this same iconography.
The '*Porta della Balla' or of the Cornacchini* (door to the West on the Northern side): the door was given this name due to its proximity to the house of the Cornacchini family.
It was build in various stages during the 14th century. The portal was completed in the 1340's and the frame, by Francesco Talenti, was built between 1359-60 and altered in 1380. Polichrome lunette with *Madonna and Child and two Angels*: the Madonna is attributed to Zanobi di Bartolo (1377-78) and the two *Angels* to Simone Talenti together with the *Madonna* of the door to the Campanile.
Lower down, on the sides, a lioness with cubs and a lion with a putto support two twisted columns on the top of which are pinnacles containing small statues, attributed to Niccolò di Pietro Lamberti and Andrea Orcagna. In the apex is the *Saviour*.

Cathedral Interior

The interior is one of the most important examples of Gothic architecture: it is in the form of a Roman cross, divided into three naves with four bays, each having mighty multiform pilasters (each pilaster has several bands). These support arches and pointed vaults with ribbing. A gallery supported by butresses runs along the length of the central nave, and continues under the dome and transept.
The floor, in polichrome marble was based on a design by Baccio d'Agnolo (1526-1660), and was continued by his son Giuliano and by Francesco da Sangallo and others. Many of the paintings which were once in the church (from the end of the thirteenth century to the beginning of the fifteenth century) are now in the Museo dell'Opera del Duomo.

INNER FAÇADE

From left to right on entering:
in the nave on the left, stained glass with *Santo Stefano and two Angels*, from a cartoon by Ghiberti, made by Niccolò di Pietro. This, together with the other two stained glass windows of the inner facade, were made between 1405 and 1415. The window re-establishes an element which was common in the 14th century and which in the fourth decade of the century became an important aspect in the decoration of the Cathedral. They also have considerable symbolic importance, as they link the exterior to the interior.
On the pilaster: *Santa Caterina d'Alessandria* and a *worshipper*, on a

Cathedral, interior

gold background, by the school of Bernardo Daddi (14th century);
on the wall: *tomb of Antonio d'Orso*, Bishop of Florence (died 1321), by Tino di Camaino. Many of the sculptures have been removed from the tomb, and are now to be found in other locations (also in foreign collections and museums), some however, can be seen in the Museo del Bargello. The tomb was the artist's second important work in Florence (1318-1323), after the tomb for Gastone della Torre in Santa Croce. The sculpture has three different levels, from lower to upper level: a corbel, sarcophagus and statue of the deceased, seated. The iconographic theme of the sepulchre is that of *Death* and the *Final Judgement*. The sarcophagus rests on three crouching lions and in the relief is portrayed Judgement at the Time of Death, an allegory of which is found in the bracket under the sarcophagus. The structure had various other elements above these, which are now missing. Among these were a canopy with two *Angels sounding Trumpets* (one of which was moved to the door of the Campanile), referring to the elevation of the spirit. One possible interpretation of the monument is the image of the spirit (the statue on the sarcophagus), at the time of resurrection (the elevation) accompanied by four angels. The coats of arms are those of the d'Orso family and Boniface VIII.
Above, beneath the vault of the central nave: glass window representing *Our Lady of the Assumption* by Niccolò di Pietro, from a cartoon by Ghiberti (1405).

Plan of the Cathedral

The *Clock* is the work of Lorenzo di Benevento della Volpaia, and has heads of prophets in the corners, painted by Paolo Uccello in 1443.
The decoration was carried out at the same time as Uccello's work on the windows around the drum of the dome. The clock face has the twenty-four hours placed radially on a painted background, in anti-clockwise sense. The division of time does not follow the regular rhythm, but instead has its point of reference at sunset, the time when the Ave Maria is sung. Since

Cathedral, interior, view of the left aisle

The inner façade, clock by Paolo Uccello

sunset changes according to the season, the longer hand indicates the hour according to the time at which it is currently set. The clock works with a pendulum and counterweights, placed at the back, and is wound every eight or nine days.

The heads are of *Prophets*, or possibly the *four Evangelists*. Stylistically they are similar to the heads in the frames of Ghiberti's Baptistery doors and to Masaccio's frescos in the Carmine church. Uccello was also responsible for the blue background of the clockface, and the gilding of the hands. The idea probably came from the clock on San Marco in Venice.

In the lunette above the portal is a mosaic of the *Enthronment of Mary*, attributed to Gaddo Gaddi (beginning of the 14th century);

to the sides of the door, within small

arches on top of columns, is a fresco by Santi di Tito with *Angels playing Music* and *Putti with Flowers*, on a gold background.
In the nave on the right: coloured stained glass of *San Lorenzo and Angels*, the work of Niccolò di Pietro from a drawing by Ghiberti.
Right Nave:
First Bay:
1. medallion with *marble bust of Brunelleschi* by Andrea di Lazzaro Cavalcanti known as 'Il Buggiano' (1446); this is a commemorative plate with an inscription written by the Chancellor of the Republic, Carlo Marsuppini. This then became the model for all other monuments in the Cathedral up until the ninteenth century;
2. *tabernacle in wood painted* in imitation of marble, by Bartolomeo Ammannati, with a marble statue of the *Prophet Daniel*, by Nanni di Banco (1408);
3. a tondo containing a *bust of Giotto working on a mosaic*, by Benedetto da Maiano (1490) and an *inscription* by Poliziano.
On the first pilaster there is a Gothic *holy water stoup* attributed to Giovanni Fetti (1380), the original Angel and bowl are now in the Opera del Duomo;
on the pilaster: pointed panel painting of Saint Anthony, by Francesco Morandini, known as 'il Poppi' (16th century) and *predella* by Antonio Marini (19th century).
Second Bay:
1. access to the crypt of Saint Reparata;
2. Saint Bartolomeo Enthroned and predella by Rossello di Jacopo Franchi;
Third Bay:
1. window with six *Saints*, from a cartoon by Agnolo Gaddi (1394);
2. *marble tabernacle* by Bartolomeo Ammannati with a statue of *Isaiah* by Bernardo Ciuffagni (1427);
3. to the sides of the tabernacle: on the right, a fresco representing the *false tomb* of the Augustinian priest, Luigi Marsili, in chiaroscuro by Bicci di Lorenzo (1439), removed and transferred to canvas in the 19th century). The deceased is portrayed lying on the sarcophagus, with a book on his chest; on the monument there is a false bas-relief of the *Three Theological Virtues*. On the left is a fresco representing the *false tomb* of Cardinal Pietro Corsini, Bishop of Florence (died 1405) in chiaroscuro by Bicci di Lorenzo (1422), removed and transferred to canvas in the 19th century. The body is in Bishop's dress, and is lying on the tomb, with the cardinal's hat at the feet. Above the tomb is the coat of arms of the Corsini family and a false bas-relief of the *Three Theological Virtues*;
Fourth Bay:
1. window with six *Saints* designed by Agnolo Gaddi (1395) and made by Antonio da Pisa;
2. *bust of Marsilio Ficino* (1433-99) by Andrea Ferrucci (1521).
The transept is composed of three large tribunes, each containing five chapels, they are lit by double light

windows with stained glass from cartoons designed mainly by Ghiberti. The overall plan for the decoration of the fifteen chapels in the choir and high altar dates from1435.
Brunelleschi and Ghiberti designed temporary wooden altars, which were then constructed by Antonio Manetti Ciaccheri. After the four double lights of the side aisles, dating from the last decade of the 14th century, the decoration of the windows was commissioned from Ghiberti in 1439 and completed in 1442. The subjects are the *Saints* to which the chapels are dedicated, and the *Prophets* in the windows above the chapels. The windows were made by: Angelo Lippi, Lorenzo d'Antonio, Guido di Niccolò, Niccolò di Piero Tedesco, Bernardo di Francesco, Guido di Niccolò, Domenico di Pietro da Pisa, Biagio di Angiolo, Francesco di Giovanni.
The frescoes on the far walls, representing the relevant saints, are the work of Bicci di Lorenzo (1439-40), except for that of the central chapel, which is by Arturo Viligiardi (1906). The figures are framed by four Corinthian columns.
The tribune on the right (Holy Conception): the name derives from a votive image of the Blessed Virgin, brought to the Cathedral in the 18th century and placed in the tribune, previously known as that of Sant'Antonio Abate. The altar with the holy image is still in the central chapel. There is also a white marble altar in this chapel, with a bronze grate, made in a style similar to that of Michelozzo. The 18th century altar in the North tribune is a companion to this.
Left chapel: *Madonna del Popolo*, a fragment of a fresco in Gothic style.
South Sacristy: above the entrance is a lunette of the *Ascension* in glazed terracotta by Luca della Robbia. This was the second made for the Cathedral, and was commissioned from the artist in 1446, completed in 1451. In comparison to the earlier one, Luca introduced coloured motifs from nature (the earth, plants and trees, details of individuals). This indicates a development in the technique of sculpted, glazed terracotta which now found itself in competition with white marble. In both lunettes the contact point of the various pieces can be seen, most of which coincide with the outline of the parts which were fired separately, and then assembled. In this way the technical problem of breakage or other damage during firing was avoided.
In 1433 the choir screen was commissioned from Donatello. It was placed over the door in 1439, and removed from there in 1688 to the building which is now the Museo dell'Opera del Duomo.
Interior: not usually open; the original plan was for decoration in wood and marble. On the left, entering, is a *lavabo* by Andrea di Lazzaro Cavalcanti, known as 'il Buggiano' (1445), in the form of a marble tympanum tabernacle with two small Corinthian pilasters (echoing the shape of the windows in the Baptistery) with two winged putti holding amphoras, a

Luca della Robbia: Ascension

design previously carried out for the lavabo in the twin (north) Sacresty. Some panels, which were originally part of the Madonna and Trinity altars in the church: the Saviour (1404), *Saints and Doctors of the Church* by Mariotto di Nardo, three *Evangelists* by Lorenzo di Bicci (all being restored at present); the *Archangel Raphael and Tobiolo* by Francesco Botticini, 1480 (not in place at present); the *Archangel Michael*, panel painting by Lorenzo di Credi (1523), with a gilded frame by Giovanni di Benedetto Cianfanini (contemporary);

CENTRAL TRIBUNE (SAN ZANOBI): the *Saints* between the columns are not frescoes but modern paintings (A. Viligiardi 1906).

Central Chapel

A civic decree of 1409 declared that San Zanobi should be honoured in suitable manner in the new cathedral. Zanobi was Bishop of Florence at the beginning of the fifth century, and had already been venerated in the crypt of the Basilica of Santa Reparata and previous to that in San Lorenzo. The location chosen was the central chapel of the eastern tribune, in line with the central aisle and the Baptistery. The project was given to Brunelleschi and Ghiberti in 1428. The two artists decided on a crypt beneath the chapel, which would be open underneath a grating to enable one to see the sarcophagus. Work began in 1432 with the stained glass windows in the most

important of the fifteen chapels, and Ghiberti was made responsible for the sarcophagus after the master builders had chosen his design from several. The *altar* in white marble is by Giuseppe Francesco Bambi. The bronze urn beneath the altar has a scene depicting the *Miracle of the Saint* in bas-relief on three sides, and on the other long side, *Angels bearing a Crown* and a latin inscription composed by the Chancellor of the Republic, Leonardo Bruni: on this side is the opening which contains the ceremonial *reliquary bust* with the head of the Saint, a masterpiece in silver of the goldsmith's art, by Andrea Arditi, with precious stones and enamel. Closed inside its box, it is only brought out on special occasions. Ghiberti's sarcophagus abandons the Gothic style of the deceased lying on top of the tomb, for that of the Classical sarcophagus. The terms of the commission for the urn imposed a limit of three and a half years, but it still had not been completed in 1437. The time was then extended to 1440. From documents we know that the two minor stories for the two ends had been begun, but that the larger one, completed in 1442, was still to be started.
On the altar there are *two angel candelsticks* in glazed terracotta (c. 1448) by Luca della Robbia, previously located in the Old Sacristy, and previous to that on the Altar of the Madonna. This pair of angels was originally destined for the chapel of Santo Stefano (dedicated to the Holy Sacrament). This is the earliest

Donatello: choir screen, in the Museo dell'Opera del Duomo

Lorenzo Ghiberti: sarcophagus of San Zanobi, detail

Luca della Robbia: Angel candle-holder

example of glazed statuary; the angels are made in one piece.
On the far wall is the *Last Supper* by Giovanni Balducci, known as 'il Cosci', whose paintings are late Mannerist in style, and in which one can detect the severity of the period of the Counter Reformation (1588).

The New Sacristy (North)

-visible through a glass door. This sacristy is famous in the history of Florence as having provided refuge for Lorenzo il Magnifico, when fleeing from the Pazzi conspiracy, in which his brother, Giuliano, lost his life (1478).
The role of these holy chambers in the 15th century and before the Council of Trent, was much more important than today. Their function has gradually changed until they are now nothing but depositaries of liturgical vestments and 'changing rooms' for the clergy to prepare themselves before the service.
On the contrary, in the 14th century and later, patronage of the sacristy was much coveted, after that of the main chapel. The entire decoration of this area was completed within forty years.
The supervisors of the furnishings of the two sacristies decided to give priority to the North one. In documents up until 1442 it is uniquely referred to, indicating that it was the only one on which they were working.
All the plans, internal and external, were based on the two sacristies being mirror images, but the north sacristy was the prototype. In April 1435 it was decided to furnish them with wooden cupboards. The first phase of the work was the construction of the wooden benches, undertaken by salaried craftsmen and master carpenters. By 1436 both these and the glass windows were completed. No trace of these furnishings has remained. The later and present arrangement is the work of various artists: the inlaid cupboards were begun by Agnolo di Lazzaro, known as 'dei Cori', on the right (south) side, in 1436-40 and by Antonio Manetti (1436-45) on the left (north) wall. They were finished by Giuliano and Benedetto da Maiano (1463-65 circa) from cartoons designed by Maso da Finiguerra (the *Annunciation*) and Alessio Baldovinetti (*Nativity* and *Circumcision*). Perspective wood inlay appeared in the 15th century, and has no real precedent in any other similar technique (marble, glass paste). The niches with still lifes have perhaps a precedent in the frescoed still lifes by Taddeo Gaddi in the Baroncelli Chapel in Santa Croce.
One can recognise the hand of Brunelleschi in the overall style and execution of the decorations. Although heavily committed in the building of the dome, choir and tribunes, he co-ordinated the design and work here, entrusting his pupils and collaborators to carry out the completion of some areas.
The whole area was systematically restored during the period from 1971-1982.

INTERIOR

The Sacristy of the Holy Mass, interior

South wall (on the right, entering): Agnolo di Lazzaro, 1436-40: above a plinth with drawers, on the lower level, in the centre, two *panels* with putti and vases of poppies and oak branches, and, surrounding, trompe l'oeil *inlay* with cupboards; on the upper level, *squares* with geometric designs and the *Lamb of God*, and illusionistic *panels* with hooks in the ceiling from which hang festoons.
North wall (on the left): Antonio Manetti 1436-45: above a plinth with drawers, on the first level, in the centre, two *panels* with vases of lilies, surrounded by trompe l'oeil *cupboards*; some of the books have pages showing music and text. On the upper level, in the centre, vases with lilies, surrounded by *panels* with decorative motifs.
East wall (opposite the entrance): Giuliano da Maiano, 1463-65: on the lower level, *San Zanobi enthroned* with his disciples *Sant'Eugenio* (on the left) and *San Crescenzio* (on the right) framed by perspective niches; to the sides, two still lifes, or illusionistic *inlays* of half open cupboards revealing liturgical accessories and books. On the upper level in the middle, an *Annunciation* and, to the sides, the prophets *Amos* and *Isaiah*, flanked by narrow panels with vases of poppies. The presence of Isaiah, with a scroll in his hand, is related to his prophecy of the birth of a virgin. On the far wall we find most of

Giuliano da Maiano: Annunciation, from a cartoon by Maso di Finiguerra

Giuliano da Maiano: Nativity, from a cartoon by Alessio Baldovinetti

Giuliano da Maiano: illusionistic inlay

Giuliano da Maiano: San Zanobi Enthroned with Sant'Eugenio and San Crescenzio

the clues to the iconographic interpretation of this area: in the centre is the *Annunciation* with two prophets to the sides; above, the image of the Bishop and Saint with his followers. In this scenographic and illusionistic setting, the central position of this scene reminds us of the religious representation of the *Annunciation* which took place in churches, (one was even designed by Brunelleschi himself), thus strongly re-enforcing the fundamental theme.
The panelling for the far wall was completed in 1465; not long afterwards, Giuliano da Maiano was commissioned to undertake the panels of the *Nativity* and the *Presentation at the Temple* for the second row on the entrance wall (west).
On this wall, on the right, entering, is a *cupboard* with wooden doors, in a marble frame which has a tympanum in which there is a sculpted angel's head (attributed to Mino da Fiesole); on the left, a *lavabo* by Andrea di Lazzaro Cavalcanti, known as 'il Buggiano' (1438-40), a marble tabernacle with tympanum and two small Corinthian pilasters, similar to that in the sacresty opposite, with two winged putti seated on a goat skin. The positions had been specified in the contract, - the *Presentation* is placed by the lavabo, and the *Nativity* by the marble cupboard. From the iconographic point of view, the two episodes follow the *Annunciation*, and they also match the theme of the stained glass windows in the roundels in the drum of

Bronze door of the Sacristy of the Holy Mass, detail

the dome, representing the *Story of the Virgin*. Confirming that the iconographic plan should be in harmony with an overall scheme, and not just within a smaller context, we can see that the position of the roundels in the drum representing the *Ascension* and the *Resurrection* is directly connected to the lunette by Della Robbia which has the same theme. Thus once more the iconography of San Zanobi is linked to the theme of the central chapel.
Above, all around the four walls, is a frieze of putti with festoons (very similar to the frieze painted by Andrea del Castagno in villa Carducci, Legnaia) sculpted in wood by the workshop of Giuliano da Maiano, and on the west wall, a garland with a *Lamb of God*.
Exterior
Bronze door by Luca della Robbia

Luca della Robbia: Choir screen, detail. Museo dell'Opera del Duomo

assisted by Michelozzo and Maso di Bartolomeo: Luca della Robbia was asked to make the door in July 1445, after it had been commissioned from Donatello who however, had too many other commissions and work also outside Florence. Thus for this work Luca joined up with Michelozzo and both were assisted by Maso di Bartolomeo, a specialist in casting who had already worked with Michelozzo. This association guaranteed Luca an introduction to the Medici family, of whom Michelozzo was a protégé. The definitive commission was assigned in 1446.

The door is divided into ten relief squares (starting from the top left): the figures of the *Madonna and Child*, *John the Baptist*, the *Four Evangelists*, the *Four Doctors of the Church*, are all flanked by two *Angels* in adoration. Around the tiles on the door frame are twenty- four projecting

Luca della Robbia: Choir screen, detail. Museo dell'Opera

heads of Prophets and Sybils of a much later date (1461-1464), made by Maso's brother, Maso having died in 1456. The door was only put into place in 1474. Lunette above the door: *Resurrection* by Luca della Robbia, commissioned in 1442 and already in place in 1444; for this work Luca provided not only the plan, but also some samples made using the technique which was specific to his workshop, and at the time was not widely known.

A Cantoria was commissioned from Luca della Robbia in 1432, and was put in place above the door in 1438. It was removed in 1688, and since 1891 has been in the Museo dell' Opera del Duomo.

LEFT TRIBUNE (SANTA CROCE): In the floor: *gnomon* or *meridian* on a bronze plate, by Paolo dal Pozzo Toscanelli (c.1450), it is connected by a hole to the light from the dome, to measure the sun's movement . The graduations were carried out by Leonardo Ximenes (1755), and it measures the position of the sun at the summer solstice, but also serves to

Luca della Robbia: Resurrection

register the stability of the dome.
First chapel: Michelangelo's *Pietà*, now in the Museo dell'Opera del Duomo, was originally here;
Second chapel: *ornamental cover*, decorated on both sides (known as Santa Reparata's polyptych) attributed to Pacino di Buonaguida with on the front, *Madonna and Child with Saints*, (on her right) *Miniato* and *Eugenio* and (on her left) *Zanobi* and *Cresenzio* (note the iconographic repetition of the three saints); on the reverse side: *Annunciation* and (on the right) *Saint John the Baptist* and *Santa Reparata* and (on the left) *Santa Maria Maddalena* and *San Nicola di Bari*, dated about 1320;
Third chapel (Santo Stefano): *marble altar* by Buggiano (1447). It was intended that this should contain numerous relics which would be visible through an altar front consisting of a quatrefoiled bronze grating, commissioned from Michelozzo (1462); Buggiano's altar consists of a table top resting on groups of four Corinthian pilasters at each corner, a highly

decorated entablature and polichrome marble panels on the other three sides. A pointed *tabernacle* in white marble, containing later relics (17th century): Buggiano made a tabernacle (of the Holy Sacrement) for the chapel of Sant'Antonio, which was dismantled and brought to this chapel.
On the left wall, the *Disciples of Emmaus* (1588) and on the right wall the *Mission of the Disciples* (1588) by Bernardino Poccetti;
Fourth chapel: *Madonna with Child* in marble by Girolamo Ticciati, probably taken from an altar in the Baptistery which had been dismantled;
Fifth chapel: *San Guiseppe* by Lorenzo di Credi.

Michelangelo Buonarroti: Pietà. Museo dell'Opera del Duomo

In the centre of the transept: against the inner sides of the pilasters which support the arches are eight large *statues of Apostles*, all by 16th century sculptors, placed in *tabernacles* designed by Ammannati; from left to right:
Saint Matthew by Vincenzo de'Rossi
Saint Philip by Giovanni Bandini
Saint James the Lesser by Giovanni Bandini
Saint John by Benedetto da Rovezzano
Saint Peter by Baccio Bandinelli
Saint Andrew by Andrea Ferrucci
Saint Thomas by Vincenzo De' Rossi
Saint James the Greater by Jacopo Sansovino

THE ORGANS

The building of the original cathedral organs was entrusted to several famous organmakers, and in 1432 Matteo da Prato was made responsible for the work which it took him fifteen years to complete. They were also worked on later by Brother Giovanni da Mercatello (fifteenth century), and Vincenzo Sormani (17th century); the open pointed arches in the pilasters of the dome which contain the organs and cantorie are neo-gothic, designed by Gaetano Baccani (1842), one of the cathedral's architects. He was also responsible for the dismantelling of the upper part of the choir. This was part of the project to restore the cathedral to its old medieval character, eliminating anything which was not in keeping with the original style.

The Choir

In 1435 a committee chose Brunelleschi's plan for the choir and high altar. This had a high octagonal parapet, inside which are two rows of wooden stalls surrounding the high altar, which is supported on small columns, made in 1439.
Brunelleschi built an octagonal wooden choir, intending to replace it with a marble one later on. Other artists too (including Donatello and Verocchio) had made plans. In 1520-21 the first choir was replaced by another one, still in wood. Baccio Bandinelli, commissioned by Great Duke Cosimo I, began work on a new choir, which continued for more than fifty years, until 1572. Assisted by Giuliano di Baccio d'Agnolo, who was responsible for the design, the main structure - the octagonal enclosure - was built, but the statues, which should all have been in marble were only partly completed, along with other reliefs in plaster. Giovanini Bandini assisted with the reliefs. The iconography was based on the Bible, and there were to be 300 reliefs of *Prophets* in the choir, however only 88 were ever completed. Some of these are signed by the artist and dated 1555. Bandinelli left a considerable number of drawings made for this work which are important for the study of his graphic activity. They demonstrate the mixture of sacred and mythological themes : *Jupiter*, or rather God the Father, Adam, represented as *Bacchus* etc., as well as studies from antique models. Evident,

however, in these powerful forms, whether wrapped in draped clothing, or nude with long curling hair, is the figure of Michelangiolo.
In 1842, as a result of a complete re-organization, twenty four of these reliefs were removed from the structure, and fifteen are now in the entrance to the Museo dell'Opera del Duomo. Other elements which belonged to the choir, like the '*Pietà*' (now in the SS. Annunziata chapel), the statue of the *Almighty* (now in the Santa Croce chapel) and some of the columns (in the Museo dell'Opera) were removed. Around the balustrade there are twenty four marble *candel-sticks*, with square bases decorated with acanthus leaves.
On the high altar: a wooden *crucifix* (1495-97) by Benedetto da Maiano.

Baccio Bandinelli: bas-relief of the choir stall, detail

The Dome

Decorated with frescoes. According to the original project, the dome should have been decorated with mosaics, in the same way as the Baptistery, but this idea was later modified. The interior was left white by Brunelleschi, and, in technical terms, ready for the scaffolding which the decoration would require.
It thus remained white for over a century until Cosimo I decided to have it decorated, and gave the task of planning the iconographic scheme to Don Vincenzo Borghini, who had previously been responsible for figurative 'inventions' for the Medici. Using classical sources as well as the New Testament and Medieval theology, he created the *Universal Judgement*, a theme already found in the Baptistery, but in a version which reflects Counter-Reformation style;
1571-74: frescoes painted by Vasari and assistants;
1578-79: frescoes painted by Zuccari and assistants, notably Passignano.
The scenes, crowded with figures, are on four levels, plus a fifth, which has figures of *Prophets*. The plan clearly reflects that of the mosaics in the Baptistery dome, with the scenes divided into rows and segments.
Around the lantern, at the highest level, Vasari painted a row of false niches which contain 24 images of the *Elders* and of the *Apocalpyse*; beneath this, are the heirarchies of Angels, the *Seraphims* (painted blue) and the *Cherubims* (ochre-yellow); in the segment on the east side, the image of *Christ in Judgement*, surrounded by the *Madonna, Saint John, Adam and Eve and Saints*.
In the other segments on this level are figures of the blessed. Under the image of Christ, the three *Theological*

Virtues: *Faith*, *Hope* and *Charity*, this last is between the other two which personify concepts no longer relevant in the afterlife. Lower, in the same section, is an allegory representing the effects of halting time and motion, with the figure of a *winged elder with an hourglass* (Father Time), in the centre, the *Seasons Asleep*, and on the right, *Death breaking the Sickle*. In the other

Dome, the frescos in the vault

sections are the images of *Hell*, which Vasari did not succeed in finishing before his death(1574).
The figures are grouped on clouds corresponding to the holes for the scaffolding, which Brunelleschi had left to be decorated. Vasari cleverly designed a couple of devils holding an open book to disguise the hole.
Most of Vasari's drawings are kept in a collection in the Louvre. They demonstrate the artist's arduous task in adapting this complex theme to a surface which had its own, natural divisions. In all, Vasari painted the figures of the *Elders*, and half of the array of angels and the chosen.
On Vasari's death, Prince Francesco I did not choose to commission either a pupil of Vasari, or a Florentine painter to complete the work, but instead an artist from the Marche, Federico Zuccari. Zuccari, who was probably recommended by Bernardo Vecchietti, a nobleman, had already worked in Rome, and had to be called from England where he was working at the time. Rather than continuing Vasari's plan and using the drawings which he had left, Zuccari preferred to change, if not the style, the character of the figures. Where Vasari had limited himself to an anonimous and impersonal description of the figures, Zuccari introduced instead a vast range of portraits which were almost caricatures. These were even more amusing as they were almost entirely for the representation of Hell. Zuccari amused himself by portraying existing

Dome, detail of the frescos in the vault

personalities among those of the *Kings of the Earth in the Presence of God*, including even Cosimo I and Francesco I de' Medici, who had commissioned the fresco. In the section to the West, among the array of the Chosen, is the group of the *People of God*, with a self portrait of the artist (signed and dated 1576). The figures of the 'flayed' are most unusual, - human figures reduced almost to skeletons, looking like examples of anatomy, found in the corners of the segments where Hell is represented. Zuccari returned to the technique of 'fresco secco' (painting on fresh plaster), as it is quicker and more

practical, and fortunately it has survived, as it is in an area which is protected from atmospheric pollution. During the last century an attempt was made to cover up the frescoes with white paint, as they were not in keeping with contemporary taste. Many artists opposed this idea. The frescoes have been restored in recent years, with the help of an immense metal framework, which is in itself a masterpiece of engineering. In fact once it has been dismantled, it is to be transferred and re-used.

The area which has suffered most damage, is that immediately beneath the lantern, for two reasons: firstly it is nearest to the exterior, and therefore suffers from the infiltration of light, damp and water, and also because Vasari used here the technique of 'fresco secco' which is less resistant than usual fresco painting, common in Tuscany, and which was used instead on the other levels.

On the inside of the lantern is an architectural decoration by Brunelleschi. Beneath the fresco runs a gallery, round which one walks when climbing the dome, before entering in between the two shells of the dome. The second part of the climb is extremely tiring (463 steps) taking one to the external gallery which runs around the lantern (107 metres high).

THE ROUNDELS IN IN THE DRUM

The eight circular windows in the drum were closed in 1413, and for many years, until 1433, were covered with the traditional linen curtains. The figure of the master glass-maker was fundamental for the creation of the windows. Documents show us that the craftsmen were employed before the artists. Ghiberti, who had already been commissioned in 1429 for the cartoons of the windows in the tribunes and naves, was again commissioned in 1433 to design the first window (*Coronation of the Virgin* for the roundel above San Zanobi's tribune). This was the first and most important window because it is on the axis of the main entrance, and because it would be the model for all the other cartoons.

In 1434 Donatello was asked to

prepare a second cartoon, for the same roundel, and this was preferred to Ghiberti's. Donatello's window created the style for the entire series, but Ghiberti, after having completed the windows for the naves, was commissioned to make the cartoons for the *Ascension*, the *Sermon in the Garden*, and the *Presentation at the Temple* (the last window to be put into place in 1445).
The completion of the series of windows occurred at a particularly important moment in Florence's religious history, - the presence of Pope Eugenius IV in the city had stimulated new architectural and religious works.

LEFT AISLE

At the beginning of the aisle, starting from the transept end, is the door where the climb up the dome begins;
fourth bay: *stained glass window*, late 14th century, from a cartoon by Agnolo Gaddi;
panel painting by Domenico di Michelino with *Dante holding open the Book of the Divine Comedy, which illuminates Florence*, dated 1465; in the middle of the painting is the mountain with steps climbing it, which represents Purgatory, with earthly Paradise above, while on the left, behind an old medieval town gate, is Hell. On the right instead, is the city of Florence, showing the finished dome, but the marble decoration of the building yet to be begun, and a Gothic spire of the old 14th century building;
pointed panel painting with gold ground, by Bicci di Lorenzo with *Saints Cosmas and Damian* (the doctor Saints, patrons of the Medici family) with a Neo-gothic, gilded frame; in the predella, *two stories of Saints*, showing their work (on the left) and their martyrdom (on the right);
third bay:
stained glass window made in 1395;
in the marble *tabernacle* by Bartolomeo Ammannati is a statue of *King David*, by Bernardo Ciuffagni for the facade (1434);
a fresco of the e*questrian monument* to John Hawkwood by Paolo Uccello.
There are many and various incidents related to the making of the cenotaph dedicated to the English commander John Hawkwood (italianized as Giovanni Acuto).
The personage portrayed was a Captain of adventure who moved to

Roundel window

Plan of the Stained Glass Windows

Designer	Subject	Maker
Donatello	*Coronation* (1434-37)	Domenico di Pietro da Pisa Angelo Lippi
Paolo Uccello	*Nativity* (1434-37)	Angelo Lippi
Paolo Uccello	*Resurrection* (1443-44)	Bernardo di Francesco
Paolo Uccello	*Annunciation*	Bernardo di Francesco
(this last was dismantled in 1828: it was opposite Donatello's window, because it indicated the beginning of the story of Christ and the Virgin; the eighth roundel is still empty)		
A. del Castagno	*Sorrowings* (1444)	unknown
Ghiberti	*Ascension* (1443-44)	Bernardo di Francesco
Ghiberti	*Sermon in the Garden* (1443-44)	Bernardo di Francesco
Ghiberti	*Presentation un The Temple* (1443-45)	Bernardo di Francesco

Italy with his mercenary troops after the Hundred Years War, remaining in the service of the Florentine Signoria from 1377 until his death in 1394. He had therefore become an institution in the life of the city, so much so that in 1393, while he was still alive, he was given the honour of a commemorative monument inside the cathedral, on the suggestion of the Humanist Coluccio

Domenico di Michelino: the Divine Comedy of Dante

Salutati. Agnolo Gaddi and Giuliano d'Arrigo (called Il Pesello) were chosen in 1495 for the work.
The equestrian memorial was to be part painted and part relief, and was also to celebrate Pietro Farnese, who had defeated Pisa, and who had died in 1363.
Documents show that Gaddi completed the work, but only thirty years later the fresco had already badly deteriorated. The project was taken up again by the Cathedral authorities and the Wool Guild, who announced a competition in July 1433. In the meantime, control of Florence passed from the Albizzi family to Cosimo de' Medici, who returned from exile in 1434. It was he who then became responsible for the completion of the project. In 1436, the Authorities debated the new work on two occasions, and Paolo Uccello was considered, being the favourite artist of the Medici. In 1436 the monument was finished and the artist was paid: his signature can be read on the frame: 'Pauli Ugielli opus'. The artist painted the memorial in monochrome (with a green ground) in order to imitate a bronze equestrian monument, instead

Domenico di Michelino: detail of the Devine Comedy of Dante

Domenico di Michelino: detail of the Devine Comedy of Dante

of a marble one: an earlier famous example of this type of monument is the group of horses in San Marco, Venice. Another famous example, though later, is perhaps the Gattamelata by Donatello in Padova. The use of space in the work demonstrates the use of Brunelleschi's perspective in a geometric and abstract style which is typical of Uccello, reducing the forms to pure mass. A degree of complexity is caused by the use of two different perspectives. The fresco has a dedication in epigraphic, roman characters: "Ioannes Acutus eques britannicus et rei miliitaris peritissimum habitus est". The ornamental frame is clearly

Paolo Ucello: Equestrian Monument to Giovanni Acuto (John Hawkwood)

Renaissance in style, and was added by Lorenzo Credi (1524) who also worked on the restoration of the fresco. This is one of the few works of Uccello which is documented, dated and signed. The loyalty of a mercenary is being celebrated, an apparently contradictory fact, as it endows the work with an exclusively political significance, as if it were a public message from the Florentine republican regime proclaimed from the walls of the most important religious building in the city. The fresco was restored in the 17th century, and again in 1842 by Giovanni Rizzoli, who moved it to the inner facade by transferring it to canvas. In 1947 it was put in its original and

Andrea del Castagno: Equestrian Monument to Niccolò da Tolentino

present position, and restored again in 1953-54;
second bay:
fresco with the *equestrian monument* to Niccolò da Tolentino, by Andrea del Castagno. Most of what has been recounted above is also valid here. As a pair for Uccello's fresco a similar monument to the commander Niccolò Marrucci da Tolentino had been planned in 1435, but had never been made.
The personage represented was in the service of Pandolfo Malatesta, and later the Florentines for whom he achieved victory in the battle of 1433

(San Romano) which is represented in the triptych of that name by Paolo Uccello, part of which is in the National Gallery of London. He was later taken prisoner by his adversary Piccinino during the Duke of Milan's war against the Pope, Florence and Venice. He died in prison on 20th March 1435, and his remains were brought to Florence and buried in the cathedral in the presence of Pope Eugenius IV. In the same year it was decided to make a marble monument, never realized. The final memorial was only begun in 1456, by Andrea del Castagno, and in it a silver shield displays the bonds of Solomon in a circle, red on a silver ground, and a golden lion rampant with a silver sword. The inscription reads: "Hic quem sublimem in equo pictum cernis Nicolaus est Tolentinus inclitus dux florentini exercitus". The history of restoration of this fresco is similar to the previous one: it was restored by Lorenzo Credi in 1524 and again in the 17th century, at the time of Cosimo III; in 1842 it was removed and restored by Antonio Marini.
Next is a *bust of the cathedral organist*, Antonio Squarcialupi, by Benedetto da Maiano (1490) with an epigram, possibly by Poliziano;
first bay: medallion with a *bust of Arnolfo di Cambio* by Ulisse Cambi (1843);
tabernacle in painted wood by Ammannati, with a marble statue of Joshua, taken from the façade of the cathedral, begun by Ciuffagni continued by Donatello (who worked on the head), and finished by Nanni di Bartolo, known as 'Il Rosso' (1415-21); *bust of Emilio de Fabris*, by Vincenzo Consani (1887);
on the first pilaster: panel painting of *San Zenobi Enthroned, trampling Pride and Cruelty, venerated by Saints Crescenzio* (with censer) and *Eugenio* (with book); in the predella, *stories of the saints*, with mircles, by Giovanni del Biondo (1400 circa).

CRYPT OF SANTA REPARATA

Between the first and second pilasters of the right aisle, is a stair which leads to the remains of the old cathedral of Santa Reparata. The excavations, which lasted from 1966 to 1973, have brought to light the structure of the original church, demolished in 1375. The old church survived the new construction thanks to the decision to raise the floor by two metres, leaving the previous one in tact. Thus some decorated walls have remained, one of which preserves intact almost an entire scene.
The basilica of Santa Reparata was a Romanesque building, much smaller than the present cathedral, with three aisles, transept and five apses, crypt and raised choir, following a fairly traditional pattern. Remains have been found of the perimeter walls and of the mosaic flooring of the primitive Early Christian basilica with columns of the IV-V century, on which the medieval structure was built.
The excavations have also brought to light many *tomb stones* with the images of 14th century personalities

such as Giovanni de' Medici, gonfalonier of Florence (1351) and of Bishop Silvestri (1313). In 1972, during the excavations, the *tomb of Filippo Brunelleschi* was discovered with an inscription on the stone which reads "corpus magni ingenii viri Philippi Brunelleschi florentini".

In the apse is a *cast of a statue* of Saint Reparata by Arnolfo di Cambio, the original of which is in the Museo dell'Opera del Duomo. Other exhibits are Roman and Early Christian relics (marbles and ceramics) and fragments of 8th and 9th century screens.

INDEX TO THE ARTISTS

GLOSSARY OF ARTISTIC AND ARCHITECTURAL TERMS

Apse- architectural structure having niches, at the end of a basilica

Double (triple) light- window having two or three mullions, divided by a column.

Graving tool- steel tool used for engraving metal.

Bay- space contained by four pilasters, with a cross vault.

Cenotaph- funereal monument, not containing the remains of the deceased.

Butress- masonry structure which supports and balances the thrust of a construction.

Crypt- area beneath the presbytery of a church, in general used to house the remains of a revered Saint.

Intrados- internal surface of an arch or vault.

Glazing- a special technique, used in the 15th century, especially by the Della Robbia workshop, to give a gloss to coloured terracotta, possibly by mixing the colours with extremely fine ground glass.

Lantern- crowning element of a cupola, which introduces the light from outside.

Pilaster-strip- demi-pilaster, with a flat trunk, placed against the wall either decoratively, or as a support.

Lunette- semi-circular areaenclosed between the architrave of a door and the arch above.

Women's gallery- loggia or gallery, above the side aisles inside a basilica.

Nave- area between two lines of columns, in a basilica.

Opus tessellatum- a Roman technique used to make flooring from small scraps of stone, usually marble.

Pluteo- balustrade used to separate areas in a church, made from panels of decorated marble.

Quatrefoil (trefoil etc.)- decoration having four (or three) 'lobes', usually in frames or windows.

Reliquary- container, usually in precious materials and much decorated, for the relics of Saints.

Rose-window- large circular window in the facade of a church.

Holy representation- religious drama, popular in Florence in the 15th century.

Serraglia- key-stone, the stone which closes the top of a vault.

Splayed jamb- oblique part of a wall, usually

around a door or window.
Tabernacle- niche or miniature temple in stone or wood which contains the Holy Sacrament or image.

Drum- circular or polyigonal wall on which a dome rests.

Inlay- technique of cutting and placing together pieces of wood, marble etc.

Atlas- male figure often found as a support for door frames or other architectural elements.

Tympanum- tri-angular shaped area between the lintel of a doorway and arch above it.

Entablature- upper horizontal part of a structure supported by columns to which link them, and support or emphasize the structure above.

Transept- nave which is perpendicular to the others in a church.

Tribune- area reserved for the presbytery in a church.

BIBLIOGRAPHY

G. C. Argan, *Il significato della cupola* in *Filippo Brunelleschi. La sua opera e il suo tempo*, atti del convegno (Firenze ottobre 1977), Firenze, Centro Di, 1980, 1, pp. 11 - 16

C. Avery, *Donatello. Catalogo completo*, Firenze, Cantini, 1991

Beck J., *Le porte del Battistero di Firenze*, Firenze, Scala, 1985

F. e S. Borsi, *Paolo Uccello*, Milano, Leonardo, 1992
E. Borsook, *Sorge la piazza del Duomo uniti in un solo volere* in *Ghiberti e la sua arte nella Firenze del '3-'400*, Firenze, Città di vita, 1979, pp. 35-42

M.G. Burresi, *Andrea, Nino e Tommaso pisani*, Milano, Electa, 1983

A. Busignani - R. Bencini, *Le chiese di Firenze. Il Battistero di San Giovanni*, Firenze, Le Lettere, 1988

A. Busignani - R.Bencini
Le chiese di Firenze. Il quartiere di San Giovanni, Firenze, Le Lettere, 1993

La cattedrale di Santa Maria del Fiore, a cura di T. Verdon, Firenze, Centro Di, 1993

Dal Battistero al Duomo, a cura di T. Verdon, Firenze, Centro Di, 1992

Donatello e i suoi. Scultura fiorentina del primo Rinascimento, catalogo della mostra, (Firenze 1986) a cura di G. Bonsanti e A.P. Darr, Milano, 1986

Il Duomo diFirenze. Documenti sulla decorazione della chiesa e del campanile tratti dall'archivio dell'Opera, per cura di Giovanni Poggi, rist. anastatica a cura di M. Haines, Firenze, ed. Medicea 1988 (ed. or. 1909)

Duomo e Battistero di Firenze, a cura di P. Sanpaolesi e M. Bucci, Firenze, Sadea-Sansoni, 1966
Firenze e dintorni, Milano, TCI, 1974

The Florence Baptistery Doors (K. Clark, D.Finn, G. Robinson), London, Thames and Hudson , 1980

A. Garzelli, *Per una lettura del Giudizio Universale nel Battistero di Firenze* in *Romanico padano, Romanico europeo* (convegno internazionale di studi, Modena-Parma, ottobre-novembre 1977), Parma, Artegrafica Silva, 1982, pp. 399-410

G. Gentilini, *I Della Robbia. La scultura invetriata nel Rinascimento*, Firenze, Cantini, 1992

M. Haines, *La sacrestia delle messe del duomo di Firenze*, Firenze, Giunti - Cassa di Risparmio, 1983

B. Klange, *I mosaici della scarsella del San Giovanni a Firenze. L'iconografia* in "Commentari", XXVI, luglio -dicembre 1975, pp. 248-258

Lorenzo Ghiberti: "materia e ragionamenti", catalogo della mostra (Firenze 1978-79), Firenze, Centro Di, 1978

Giuseppe Marchini, *Il Battistero, il Duomo e il Museo dell'Opera del Duomo di Firenze*, Firenze, Becocci-Scala, 1972

G . Morolli, *Analecta architecturae: torri dei venti e datteri salomonici nell'architettura brunelleschiana*, pt. 1, in "Artista", 1989, 1, p. 38-51

G. Morolli, *Brunelleschi e l'arredo umanistico di Santa Maria del Fiore* in *Filippo Brunelleschi. La sua opera e il suo tempo*, atti del convegno (Firenze ottobre 1977), Firenze, Centro Di, 1980, 2, pp. 603-623

I mosaici del Battistero di Firenze, (Antony de Witt), 5 voll., Firenze, Cassa di Risparmio, 1954
L'oro del Ghiberti. Restauri alla porta del Paradiso,

Firenze, Museo Opificio delle pietre dure..., 1985-1986, stampa COPTIP Modena (opuscolo pubblicato in occasione della mostra di tre formelle restaurate)

M. Preti, *Museo dell'Opera del Duomo di Firenze*, Milano, Electa, 1989

A. M. Romanini, *La cattedrale gotica: il caso di Arnolfo a Santa Maria del Fiore* in *Storia dell'arte italiana*, Torino, Einaudi, 1983, vol. XII, pp. 5-45